A Little English Book of Teas

Rosa Mashiter

ILLUSTRATED BY MILANDA LOPEZ

First published in 1989 by The Appletree
Press Ltd, 7 James Street South,
Belfast BT2 8DL. Text © Rosa Mashiter, 1989.
Illustrations © Milanda Lopez,
1989. Printed in the U.K. All rights
reserved. No part of this publication may
be reproduced or transmitted in any form
or by any means, electronic or mechanical,
photocopying, recording or any information
and retrieval system, without permission in
writing from the publisher.

First published in the United States in 1989
by Chronicle Books, 275 Fifth Street,
San Francisco, CA 94103
ISBN 0-87701-622-4

9 8 7 6 5 4 3 2 1

A note on measures

Imperial, metric and American measures have
been used in this book. Use one set of measures
only. Where no American measure has been
used, as in the case of meat weights, please use
the metric measure. All spoon measurements are
level rather than heaped.

Introduction

Afternoon teas first became popular and fashionable in Victorian times. Although it was only considered as a light refreshment between lunch and dinner, afternoon tea was quite a serious occasion, and society ladies, such as Lady Hamilton, were renowned for their prowess at tea-making. Usually served in the drawing room between the hours of four and five o'clock, the taste and refinement of the hostess would be judged by the quality and manner in which she served her afternoon tea. There would be a selection of dainty little sandwiches, filled with wafer thin cucumber or perhaps some home-potted meat; fancy biscuits, which had to be dry in texture so as not to soil the guests' fingers; and various delicious cakes, baked below stairs by the cook. All were presented and served on the finest and most delicate of bone china, with tiny silver teaspoons and tea served from a silver teapot.

Country afternoon teas contrasted quite strongly with high society: farmhouse teas with home-baked crusty bread, thickly sliced and buttered; home cured hams, tongues and cheeses; a good, wholesome fruit cake; and scones spread thickly with clotted cream.

Tea-time is still a great English tradition, one that will endure for future generations, to be enjoyed and savoured whether it is in the regal splendour of the famous Savoy Hotel in London, the cosiness of a farmhouse kitchen, or on the green grass of an English village green, watching the local cricket match on a summer afternoon.

A 'Potted' History of Tea

Tea did not become really popular in England until the mid-eighteenth century when it arrived from China, together with teapots and elegant tea-services known as 'china'. It was not until the 1820s, when the political and commercial situation in China was giving cause for alarm, that tea-planting in India was considered. Tea had already been discovered growing there, and by the turn of the century tea had become a major Indian export. Most teas used today are blended from a variety of leaves but for the purist one of the following might be chosen:

Assam A strong Indian tea, that should be served with milk.

Darjeeling A delicious and fine tea with a delicate flavour.

Earl Grey Named after the 2nd Earl Grey who brought it back from China in 1830, it is a blend of China and Darjeeling teas, scented with oil of Bergamot.

Lapsang Souchong A pungent large-leafed China tea, always taken with lemon rather than milk.

Everybody has their own way of making tea, but it is important to use fresh water, and to warm the pot. I like to allow one teaspoon of tea per person plus one for the pot, and to let the tea stand for a good five minutes before pouring. If taking milk, I like to put the milk in first. This custom stems from the use of very thin china cups, when the hot tea could crack the cup if poured in before the milk.

English Tea~Time Sandwiches

Invented by the Earl of Sandwich in the eighteenth century, the English tea-time sandwich has become a well-established tradition.

It is far better to use bread that is a day old, for to obtain the really elegant English tea-time sandwich it is necessary to use very thinly sliced bread – either white or brown, and remove crusts once the sandwiches have been filled.

Cucumber Sandwiches

It is necessary to sweat the cucumber beforehand to avoid ending up with soggy sandwiches.

cucumber	thinly sliced bread
vinegar	butter
salt	

Peel and very thinly slice some cucumber, put the slices into a colander sitting on a deep plate, sprinkle a little vinegar and some salt all over and leave for 30-40 minutes. Shake the colander to remove any excess liquid and pat the cucumber slices dry with kitchen paper.

Lightly butter the bread, arrange an overlapping layer of cucumber on top, cover with another slice of lightly buttered bread, and press the two together firmly. Trim off the crusts with a sharp knife and cut into four triangles. Pile neatly onto a plate, covered with a lacy doily, and serve at once.

Egg and Cress Sandwiches

2 hard boiled eggs	*softened butter*
1 tsp mayonnaise	*thinly sliced bread*
salt and pepper	*cress*

Shell the eggs and chop roughly into a food processor, then add the mayonnaise, and some of the cress snipped off with scissors. Season with salt and pepper and process to mix (there should still be a good texture).

Spread the mixture on some lightly buttered bread, top with another slice, press lightly together, trim off the crusts and cut the sandwich into three fingers. Arrange on a pretty serving plate.

Potted Meat Sandwiches

left over roast beef	*pinch of ground mace*
softened butter	*thinly sliced white or*
salt and freshly ground	*brown bread*
black pepper	

Finely mince the beef in a food processor and add enough softened butter to bind together. Season with salt and pepper and a pinch of mace. Lightly butter the bread and spread the potted meat in an even, reasonably generous layer. Top with a second slice of bread, press lightly together, trim off the crusts and cut into neat fingers.

Tomato Sandwiches

ripe, but firm tomatoes	*salt and pepper*

thinly sliced, buttered white or brown bread

Put the tomatoes, stalks removed, into a basin, cover with boiling water, let stand for 1 minute then slide off the skins. Pat dry with kitchen paper, then cut the tomatoes into thin slices, and arrange on slices of buttered bread. Season with a little salt and pepper, cover with a second slice of bread and press down firmly. Trim off the crusts and cut into triangles. Pile neatly onto a serving plate and cover with a slightly dampened tea-cloth until ready to serve.

Smoked Salmon Pinwheels

These very elegant little sandwiches should be served for special occasion teas, such as christenings and weddings.

5 or 6 thin slices of soft brown bread, crusts removed	*1 tbsp very finely chopped fresh parsley*
6 oz/150 g/1 cup low fat cream cheese	*1 tbsp very finely chopped watercress*
1 ½ tbsp lemon juice	*black pepper* *pinch cayenne pepper*

Using a rolling pin slightly flatten and stretch the bread. Cream the cheese, lemon juice, parsley and watercress together, mixing in the seasonings. Spread the mixture evenly over the bread, cover with the slices of smoked salmon and very carefully roll up firmly.

Wrap each roll in foil, or cling film, and refrigerate for at least 2 hours to chill well. Remove the wrapping and cut each roll, using a sharp knife, into 5-6 slices.

To serve, arrange the pinwheels on a fine bone sandwich plate and garnish with a generous sprig of watercress and a twist of lemon.

Lancashire Cheese Scones

These little scones make a delightful savoury, and you can ring the changes by using cheese from different regions, such as Cheddar, Wensleydale, or Cheshire. Serve them warm, split and lightly buttered.

6 oz/150 g/1½ cups self-raising flour	1 egg
	a little milk
1 oz/25 g/2 tbsp margarine	pinch of salt
	pinch of cayenne
4 oz/100 g/½ cup Lancashire cheese, grated	pepper
	a little beaten egg

Put the flour and margarine into the food processor and process until the mixture resembles coarse breadcrumbs. Add the cheese, salt and cayenne and process to mix – just a few seconds. With the machine switched on add the egg, together with just enough milk to make a soft pliable dough. Roll out on a lightly floured board and cut into rounds using a pastry cutter. Place on a greased baking tray, brush with beaten egg, and bake for about 20 minutes at gas mark 7, 425°F, 200°C.

Devonshire Splits

Traditionally these little buns are served with West Country clotted cream and home-made strawberry jam. Served with a pot of tea this would be called a cream tea in the West Country.

1 lb/450 g/4½ cups strong plain flour	1 oz/25 g/2 tbsp melted butter
½ tsp salt	½ pt/300 ml/1¼ cups warm milk
2 tsp dried yeast	
1 tsp sugar	

Sieve flour and salt into a mixing bowl. Heat the milk until tepid, stir in the sugar and sprinkle the yeast on top. Leave in a warm place for 15 minutes, when it should be frothy. Make a well in the centre of the flour, pour in the yeast liquid and melted butter and using a wooden spoon mix to a soft dough. Turn onto a floured board and knead for 8-10 minutes. Put in a clean bowl, cover with clingfilm and leave to stand until doubled in size.

Cut the dough into twelve even-sized pieces, knead each piece into a ball, flatten into a round about ½ inch thick and place on a lightly greased and warmed baking tray. Cover with a cloth and stand in a warm place for 20 minutes.

Bake at gas mark 7, 425°F, 220°C for 15-20 minutes. Remove from the oven and cool on a wire rack, before splitting and spreading with clotted cream and strawberry jam.

Clotted Cream

It is believed that it was the Phoenicians, in search of tin, who first brought clotted cream to Cornwall, and thence to Devon. The clotted cream from Cornwall varies from the rich, yellow cream of Devon, in that it has a delicious buttery yellow crust on top, and its consistency is thicker. It is usually made with whole cream (whereas the Devonshire variety is made with creamy milk). A bowl of settled cream is put into a pan of hot water before being scalded. The pan is then removed from the heat and let stand for at least 24 hours in a cool place. The crusty cream will have settled on the top of the pan, and can be easily removed with a large slotted spoon. The skimmed, or buttermilk left below the cream is put to good use in soups or sauces.

Banana and Walnut Loaf

This is a lovely moist cake, with good keeping qualities. It is eaten sliced, with or without butter.

4 oz/100 g/½ cup margarine	2 oz/50 g/½ cup chopped walnuts
6 oz/175 g/¾ cup muscovado sugar	8 oz/250 g/2¼ cups self-raising flour
2 eggs	1 tsp baking powder
2 ripe bananas	2 tbsp milk

Grease and line a 2 lb loaf tin, and preheat the oven to gas

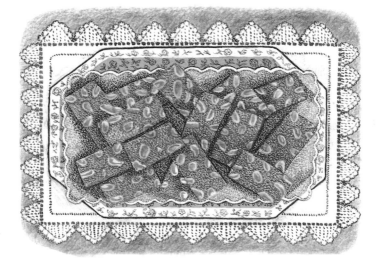

mark 4, 350°F, 180°C. Cream the margarine and sugar together. Mash the bananas and add to the mixture. Break the eggs, one at a time, into the mixture, beating well between each addition. Gently fold in the flour and baking powder and then stir in the walnuts and milk. Transfer the mixture into the loaf tin, smoothing the top, and bake for approximately one hour, or until well risen and golden brown. Turn out and cool on a wire rack.

Almond Biscuits

3 oz/75 g/¾ cup self-raising flour
1½ oz/40 g/⅓ cup butter
2 oz/50 g/⅓ cup ground almonds
1 tbsp caster sugar
a few flaked almonds

Sieve the flour into a bowl, and rub the butter in with the fingertips until the mixture resembles fine breadcrumbs. Stir in the ground almonds and caster sugar, adding a little milk, to form a soft dough.

Roll the dough out on a lightly floured board, to a rectangle about 7 inches (18 cm) square and place on a greased baking sheet. Brush with a little milk and sprinkle over a few flaked almonds. Bake for 15-20 minutes at gas mark 5, 375°F, 190°C. Immediately they come out of the oven cut into fingers, then allow to cool.

Crumpets

These delicious round 'holey' scones are excellent served freshly cooked, spread with butter and jam.

1 lb/450 g/4½ cups strong plain flour	1 pt/600 ml/2 cups water and milk mixed
½ oz/13 g/1 tbsp yeast	1 tsp salt

Heat the water and milk mixture until just tepid and remove from heat. Dissolve the yeast in a little of the warm liquid. Put the flour and salt into a large bowl, make a well in the centre, and pour in the yeast and remaining liquid, mixing well with a wooden spoon. Cover the bowl with cling film, and keep in a warm place until the mixture rises (you may need to add a little more warm milk to ensure a batter consistency).

Heat a lightly greased cast iron griddle and place the greased, metal crumpet rings on top. Spoon in some of the mixture, to about half way up the rings, and cook until bubbles form on the top, then remove the rings and cook for a further couple of minutes, until the underside is lightly browned.

If you have not got any crumpet rings, you can use egg rings, or alternatively spoon the mixture directly onto the griddle. The crumpets will be thinner, but just as delicious.

Northumberland 'Singin' Hinny'

These little flat cakes make a 'singing' noise as they cook on the griddle, and the word 'hinnie' is a term of endearment usually used by mothers in the north of England when speaking to young children who, when waiting for their teas, would pester their mothers as to whether it was ready or not, and as the little cakes would be cooking away she would answer them by saying, 'No, no, they're not ready yet, just singin', hinny.'

2 oz/50 g/4 tbsp lard	2 oz/50 g/4 tbsp caster
12 oz/375 g/2½ cups	sugar
self-raising flour	3 oz/75 g/6 tbsp currants
1 tsp salt	½ pt/300 ml/¾ cup milk
	and cream mixed

Sieve the flour and salt into a large mixing bowl, rub the fat into the flour using your fingertips, and stir in the sugar and currants. Make a well in the centre, and pour in the milk and cream mixture. With a wooden spoon slowly draw dry ingredients into the liquid to form a soft dough, finally working with your fingers. Roll the dough out on a lightly floured board to about ¼ inch thick and prick all over with a fork. Cut into quarters and place on a moderately hot griddle and cook for about 4 minutes each side, until nicely browned. Serve hot, cut in two and buttered.

Florentines

These very elegant and delicious biscuits take a little time, but are superb.

2 oz/50 g/4 tbsp butter	2 oz/50 g/½ cup chopped walnuts
4 oz/100 g/½ cup soft dark brown sugar	a few pieces of angelica
2 oz/50 g/¼ cup glacé cherries	1 tbsp sultanas
1 egg	2 oz/50 g/¾ cup desiccated coconut
4 oz/100 g/1 cup mixed peel	4 oz/100 g plain dark chocolate

Beat the butter and sugar together and beat in the egg. Roughly chop the glacé cherries and angelica and add to the egg mixture together with the mixed peel, walnuts, sultanas and coconut. Mix well.

Put teaspoonfuls of the mixture onto a baking sheet which has been covered with lightly greased cooking parchment. Space the spoonfuls reasonably apart as the biscuits will spread out as they cook. Bake at gas mark 4, 350°F, 180°C for about 25 minutes.

Remove from the oven and leave on the baking tray for about 10 minutes to harden. Carefully transfer to a wire rack to cool.

Melt the chocolate over a bowl of hot water, and drizzle teaspoons over each biscuit. Allow to set.

Bath Buns

Cobb's, founded by James Cobb in 1866 in Bath, have been making these delectable little buns from an old recipe of 1679 to this day. They are served in the Pump Room at Bath and are a delight not to be missed, with their distinctive sugared top

1 lb/450 g/4½ cups strong plain flour	4 oz/100 g/½ cup caster sugar
1 oz/25 g fresh yeast	6 oz/150 g/¾ cup butter
1 tsp sugar	3 eggs, beaten
300 ml/½ pt/1cup milk and water mixed	crushed sugar lumps for topping
pinch salt	

Put a third of the flour into a large mixing bowl, crumble in the yeast and add 1 teaspoon sugar and a pinch of salt. Heat the water and milk mixture until just tepid and pour over the dry ingredients. Mix well, and leave to stand in a warm place for about half an hour. Meanwhile soften the butter and beat with the eggs until light and creamy. Add to the mixing bowl with the remaining flour and sugar. Turn onto a floured board and knead until smooth, then put into a bowl, cover with cling film, and leave to rise until doubled in size.

When ready knead again and divide into 15 or 16 slightly flattened balls and place on a greased baking tray. Cover again and allow to prove, for about 30 minutes.

Brush the buns with a little beaten egg and sprinkle the crushed sugar cubes over the top.

Bake at gas mark 6, 400°F, 200°C for 15-20 minutes, or until golden brown. Serve split and buttered.

Maids of Honour

These little tartlets are said to have originated at the court of Henry VIII, when he chanced one day upon some of the Queen's maids of honour eating cakes. Being famous for his voracity, he could not resist the temptation to try one himself, and found them so delicious he named them Maids of Honour.

8 oz/250 g/1⅓ cups curd cheese	*1 oz/25 g/¼ cup ground almonds*
3 oz/75 g/6 tbsp softened butter	*pinch of ground nutmeg*
2 eggs	*a few flaked almonds*
1 tbsp brandy	*8 oz/250 g packet of puff pastry*
2 tbsp caster sugar	

Roll the puff pastry out on a lightly floured board and use to line 12 lightly greased bun tins. Mix together all the remaining ingredients, except the flaked almonds, and spoon into the pastry cases. Sprinkle a few flaked almonds on each and then bake at gas mark 7, 425°F, 220°C for 15-20 minutes until the pastry is golden brown and the filling is set.

Chelsea Buns

A favourite of George III, and so named because they were sold from the Old Chelsea Bun House.

---

12 oz/375 g/3 cups plain flour	1 tsp salt
	1 egg
6 oz/150 g/¾ cup soft brown sugar	½ pt/240 ml/1 cup milk and water mixed
2 oz/50 g/4 tbsp margarine	1 oz/25 g/2 tbsp butter, melted
⅓ oz/10 g/2 tsp dried yeast	8 oz/250 g/1½ cups mixed dried fruit

Glaze

2 tbsp caster sugar	4 tbsp boiling water

Heat the milk until tepid, sprinkle over the yeast and stand in a warm place for 20 minutes, when it should be frothy. Put the flour and salt into a bowl and rub in the margarine with your fingertips until the mixture resembles fine breadcrumbs. Stir in a third of the brown sugar. Add the milk mixture and beaten egg and mix to form a pliable dough. Turn onto a floured board and knead for 4 minutes, then put into a clean bowl, cover with cling-form film and stand until the dough has doubled in size.

Turn onto a floured board, knead again lightly, and roll out to a rectangle 20 in x 8 in (50 cm x 20 cm). Brush with melted butter, sprinkle with mixed fruit and remaining brown sugar, and roll up from the longest side to form a

Swiss Roll shape. Cut into 12 slices and place cut side down in a deep, lightly greased and warmed tin. Cover with a cloth and leave in a warm place until doubled in size (about 30 minutes). Bake at gas mark 6, 400°F, 200°C for 20 minutes. Remove from the tin and cool on a rack. Dissolve the sugar in the boiling water and brush all over the top and sides of the buns. Leave to cool completely.

Melting Moments

My late mother-in-law was an excellent baker who enjoyed nothing more than setting a day aside each week to bake an assortment of cakes, biscuits, scones, buns and bread, and I enjoyed many delicious tea-times with her. Melting Moments were among her favourites, delicious little confections that really do melt in the mouth.

5 oz/125 g/1¼ cups self-raising flour	1 egg
2½ oz/65 g/5 tbsp lard	few drops vanilla essence
3 oz/75 g/6 tbsp sugar	crushed cornflakes or desiccated coconut

Cream the fat and sugar together until light and fluffy, then add the egg and beat well. Fold in the flour and vanilla essence. Roll the mixture into small balls the size of walnuts, then roll in crushed cornflakes (or desiccated coconut), place on a greased baking sheet and bake for 10 minutes only at gas mark 5, 375°F, 190°C.

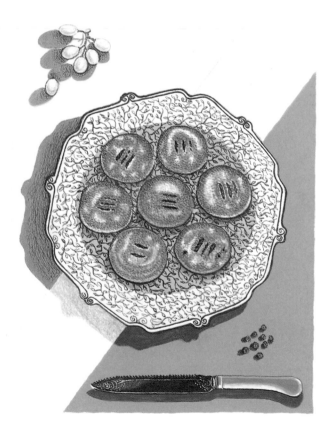

Banbury Cakes

When I moved to the West Country many years ago, I found that on visits to my parents, who lived on the Oxfordshire/Buckinghamshire border I had to drive through Banbury, famous for its cross and for its little cakes. Sadly the cake shop I used to visit has long gone but you can still enjoy Banbury Cakes in the local tea shop and in some of the pubs.

1 lb/450 g frozen puff pastry, defrosted	1 oz/25 g/¼ cup mixed peel
2 oz/50 g/4 tbsp butter	½ tsp allspice
3 oz/75 g/6 tbsp soft brown sugar	½ tsp ground cinnamon
4 oz/100 g/⅔ cup currants	1 tbsp rum
	beaten egg
	caster sugar

Roll out the pastry on a well-floured board and using a tea plate as a guide cut out 6-8 circles. Mix all the remaining ingredients together, except the beaten egg and caster sugar, and divide equally among the pastry rounds. Dampen all round the edges with water, then draw up over the filling and seal in the centre; lightly flatten. Place the cakes, seal side down on a greased baking sheet and make three little slits on the top. Bake at gas mark 7, 450°F, 220°C for 20 minutes. Just before the cakes are ready brush with a little egg and sprinkle over a little sugar then return to the oven for a few minutes.

Porterhouse Plum Cake

Although called a plum cake, it does not in fact contain plums but nuts and raisins, and I find that the addition of grapefruit gives it a distinctive tangy flavour.

1 lb/450 g/2⅔ cups raisins	2 oz/50 g/4 tbsp butter
2 fl oz/60 ml/4 tbsp water	2 oz/50 g/4 tbsp caster sugar
2 fresh grapefruits	4 oz/100 g/1 cup chopped almonds
12 oz/375 g/3½ cups self-raising flour	3 tbsp milk
1 tsp baking powder	2 eggs

Stone and roughly chop the raisins and put into a pan of water over a gentle heat.

Squeeze all the juice from one of the grapefruits, and finely grate the rind. Peel the second grapefruit and segment the flesh, removing all the pith and seeds, then roughly chop the flesh.

Put the flour and baking powder into a mixing bowl and rub in the butter. Stir in the sugar and chopped nuts and mix well. Add the raisin mixture, milk, grapefruit juice and eggs, mix in the grapefruit rind and flesh.

Pour into a large greased and lined 8-inch (20 cm) square tin and cook at gas mark 4, 350°F, 180°C for about an hour, or until golden brown. Turn out and cool on a wire rack. Dredge the top with caster sugar.

Simnel Cake

When young girls went into domestic service, this cake was baked for Mothering Sunday, the only day in the year when they were allowed home. The girls demonstrated the cooking skills they had learnt by taking with them a rich fruit cake, decorated with almond paste, called a Simnel Cake. Later the cake became popular at Easter when it was decorated with eleven marzipan balls, symbolizing the faithful disciples, and tied with a satin ribbon.

---

8 oz/250 g/1¼ cups plain flour
6 oz/150 g/12 tbsp soft brown sugar
6 oz/150 g/¾ cup margarine
4 eggs

1 tsp ground cinnamon
12 oz/375 g/2 cups currants
4 oz/100 g/8 tbsp sultanas
3 oz/75 g/6 tbsp mixed peel
8 oz/250 g marzipan

Decoration

1 lb/450 g marzipan
3 tbsp apricot jam

1 egg white

Line and lightly grease an 8-inch (20 cm) round cake tin. Roll the 8 oz marzipan to a 7½-inch (17 cm) circle. Cream the margarine and sugar until light and fluffy, then beat in the eggs, one at a time. Put the flour, cinnamon and dried fruit into a large bowl and mix well. Fold half of the dry ingredients into the egg, fat and sugar mixture with a metal spoon. When thoroughly mixed fold in the remaining half. Put half the cake mixture into the tin, and level with a palette knife, then lay the circle of marzipan on the top. Carefully top with the remaining cake mixture, smoothing the top level, then making a shallow well in the centre to enable the cake to rise evenly.

Bake at gas mark 3, 325°F, 160°C for 2 hours. When cooked remove from the tin onto a wire cooling rack and leave the cake to become cold before decorating.

Divide the marzipan into two pieces. Roll out one half to fit the top of the cake. Roll the other half of marzipan into eleven individual little balls.

Put the apricot jam into a small saucepan and heat gently, then strain through a sieve. Spread over the top of the cake and press the large piece of marzipan firmly on top. Crimp the edges of the marzipan all the way round with thumb and forefinger of your left hand and the forefinger of your right. Lightly beat the egg white and use a little to secure the balls firmly and evenly around the edge of the top of the cake. Then brush all over the top of the cake with egg white and put under a hot grill for 1-2 minutes only, until only the marzipan is well browned.

Jam Tart

4 oz/100 g/1 cup plain flour
2 oz/50 g/4 tbsp margarine

1 oz/25 g/2 tbsp caster sugar
water   6 tbsp jam

Put the flour into a large mixing bowl and rub in the margarine, using your fingertips, until the mixture resembles fine breadcrumbs. Stir in the sugar and add enough water to form a firm dough. Roll out on a lightly floured board and use to line an 8 inch (20 cm) flan dish. Spread the jam over the base, and decorate with thin strips of pastry in a lattice design. Bake at gas mark 5, 400°F, 200°C for 30 minutes, until the pastry is golden brown.

Rock Cakes

The mixture is spooned into rough, rocky shapes before baking, hence the name.

---

8 oz/250 g/2¼ cups self-raising flour	*4 oz/100 g/½ cup caster sugar*
4 oz/100 g/½ cup margarine	*4 oz/100 g/⅔ cup mixed dried fruit*
1 egg	*1 tbsp milk*

Put the flour and margarine, cut up in small pieces, in a large mixing bowl and using the fingertips rub the fat into the flour, until the mixture resembles coarse breadcrumbs. Add the sugar and dried fruits and mix well. Beat the egg and stir into the mixture together with the milk to give a stiff dough. Spoon the mixture into small rocky-shaped piles on a greased baking tray.

Bake at gas mark 6, 400°F, 200°C for about 15 minutes, when the cakes will be golden brown and firm to the touch. Remove from the baking tray, using a palette knife, and cool on a wire rack.

Gingerbread

Gingerbread was a great favourite of the poet William Wordsworth, usually made by his sister Dorothy.

---

8 oz/250 g/2¼ cups plain flour
4 oz/100 g/½ cup butter
5 oz/125 g/10 tbsp muscovado sugar
2 tsp ground ginger   pinch of ground cinnamon

Put the flour and spices into a mixing bowl and rub in the butter, using your fingertips, until the mixture resembles fine breadcrumbs. Stir in the sugar, using a little water, and mix to a firm dough. Press firmly into a lined and lightly greased square tin (the mixture should be about ½ inch thick). Bake at gas mark 3, 325°F, 160°C for about 30 minutes. Remove from the oven and cool on a wire tray, then cut into fingers.

To make gingerbread men, make as above, but roll out on a lightly floured board to about ¼ inch thick, and using a special gingerbread men cutter, cut out the men. Place on a greased baking sheet and bake for about 15-20 minutes. When cooked, cool on a wire rack then, using an icing bag, pipe on the faces and buttons down the front.

Farmhouse Fruit Cake

Wholemeal flour is used in this cake, which gives it a distinctive nutty flavour. A nice thick slab, served with a piping hot mug of tea at a scrubbed pine table in a farmhouse kitchen has to be simple fare at its best.

8 oz/250 g/1 cup butter or margarine, softened	12 oz/350 g/3½ cups wholemeal self-raising flour
8 oz/250 g/1 cup soft brown sugar	1½ lbs/675 g/4 cups mixed dried fruit
4 eggs	4 oz/100 g/½ cup glacé cherries
2 tsp mixed spice	
grated rind of a lemon	4 oz/100 g/1 cup chopped nuts
grated rind of an orange	
2 tbsp sherry	

Beat the butter and sugar together in a large mixing bowl until pale and creamy. Beat in the eggs, one at a time, adding a tablespoon of flour with each egg. Beat in the mixed spice, orange and lemon rinds. Fold in the remaining flour with the fruit, cherries and nuts, and stir in the sherry to give a smooth dropping consistency. Spoon the mixture into a greased and lined 8-inch (20 cm) round cake tin, and level the top of the cake with a palette knife.

Bake for 2-3 hours at gas mark 2, 300°F, 150°C until golden brown and firm to touch. Leave to cool in the tin before turning out.

Marika's Marmalade Cake

This delicious cake was created by the late Marika Hanbury Tenison, who was one of England's most loved and respected cookery writers. Marika would have been the first person to admit that cakes and baking were not a part of cookery that she really enjoyed, but needs be. One afternoon she had unexpected visitors for tea at her beautiful seventeenth-century farmhouse on the top of Bodmin Moor in Cornwall. This cake was the end result of a mad dash to get a presentable tea together in the shortest possible time.

---

8 oz/250 g/2¼ cups self-raising flour	3 tbsp cider (or apple juice)
5 oz/125 g/10 tbsp soft brown sugar	3 tbsp marmalade
4 oz/100 g/8 tbsp butter	6 oz/150 g/1 cup mixed dried fruit
2 large eggs	2 oz/50 g/¼ cup glacé cherries

This cake is made in a food processor, or you can use a food mixer. Put the flour, sugar, butter and eggs into the processor and mix until you have a nice smooth dough, then add the marmalade and cider and process again. Add the fruit and glacé cherries and just process to mix. Put the mixture into a greased and lined loaf tin and bake for 1 hour at gas mark 4, 350°F, 180°C. When the cake is ready, leave it in the tin for 15-20 minutes before turning it out on a wire rack to cool.

Victoria Sponge

Named after Queen Victoria, this is a delicious light-as-air sponge made in two layers and sandwiched together with a filling of raspberry jam and buttercream.

3 eggs	6 oz/150 g/¾ cup butter
6 oz/150 g/¾ cup caster sugar	6 oz/150 g/1½ cups self-raising flour

Filling

3 tbsp jam	6 oz/150 g/¾ cup icing (confectioners) sugar
3 oz/75 g/⅔ cup butter	
2 tbsp warm water	

Lightly grease and line base of 2 x 7-inch (18 cm) round sandwich tins. Beat the butter and sugar together in a bowl until pale and creamy. Beat in the eggs, one at a time, adding a tablespoon of flour with each egg. Fold in the remaining flour. Divide the mixture equally between the two tins and bake at gas mark 4, 350°F, 180°C for about 20 minutes until well risen, golden brown and firm to touch in the centre. Remove from the oven and allow to cool for about ten minutes before turning out onto a wire cooling rack. To make the buttercream, soften the butter, gradually beat in the sugar, and finally beat in the water.

Spread the base of one cake with the jam then carefully spread the buttercream on top. Place the other cake on top, and press down lightly. Sprinkle a little more icing sugar on top.

Rich Chocolate Cake

6 oz/150 g/1¾ cups self-raising flour	2 large eggs, separated
	6 tbsp each water/oil
6 oz/150 g/¾ cup caster sugar	1 tbsp rum
	1½ oz/40 g/2 tbsp cocoa

Filling

3 oz/75 g/6 tbsp butter	a few drops vanilla
6 oz/150 g/¾ cup icing sugar	essence
	2 tbsp warm water

Icing

4 oz/100 g/½ cup icing sugar	2 tsp cocoa
	warm water

Put the flour, cocoa, oil, rum and egg yolks into a large mixing bowl and beat well with a wooden spoon. Whisk the egg whites until stiff then, using a metal spoon, fold into the chocolate mixture. Divide the mixture between two 8-inch (20 cm) sandwich tins and bake at gas mark 4, 350°F, 180°C for about 35 minutes. Remove from the oven and cool on a wire rack.

To make the filling, beat the batter and sifted icing sugar together with a tablespoon or two of warm water and one or two drops of vanilla essence until smooth. Use to sandwich the two cakes together.

Dissolve the cocoa in a tablespoon of hot water. Sift the icing sugar into a bowl and beat in the cocoa mixture, adding a little more warm water. The icing should only be

thick enough to coat the back of a spoon. When the right consistency has been achieved, spread the icing on top.

Fresh Strawberry Ice~Cream

Strawberries and cream are synonymous with the English summertime. Eton, England's most famous school, has its own way of eating fresh strawberries and cream: the fruit are mashed with double cream and sugar. It has the lovely name 'Eton Mess'! Ice-cream, however, is a very popular teatime treat, especially for children, and home-made, with home-grown fruit, it is even more delicious.

---

8 oz/250 g/1¼ cups fresh strawberries, hulled
2 eggs
¼ pt/125 ml/½ cup double or whipping cream
3 oz/75 g/6 tbsp icing (confectioners) sugar

Wash and dry the strawberries and purée in a food processor or liquidizor. Do not overprocess – leave some texture. Separate the two eggs and beat the egg yolks in a small bowl. Whisk the egg whites until stiff and gradually beat in the sugar, a spoonful at a time. Lightly whip the cream. Add the beaten egg yolks, whipped cream and puréed fruit to the egg whites, folding in lightly. Pour the mixture into a plastic container and freeze.

Remove from the freezer 10 minutes before serving and serve in glass goblets topped with a fresh strawberry and a sprig of fresh mint.

Brown Bread Ice-Cream

The distinctive 'nutty' flavour of this ice-cream makes it very popular with adults as well as children. Traditionally English, it is delicious served with fresh summer fruits.

½ pt/300 ml/1¼ cups double cream
¼ pt/150 ml/⅔ cup single cream
3 oz/75 g/6 tbsp icing (confectioners) sugar
4 oz/100 g/2 cups brown breadcrumbs
1 tbsp rum and 2 eggs

Whisk the double cream until stiff then gradually whisk in the single cream. Fold in the icing sugar and breadcrumbs. Separate the eggs, mix the yolks with the rum, and fold into the ice-cream mixture. Whisk the egg whites until stiff and fold into the mixture. Pour into freezing trays or a plastic container and freeze until firm.

Jam and Jellies

One of the English housewife's summer chores is to stock up her store-cupboard for the winter with jams, jellies and preserves, made either from fruit and vegetables grown in her kitchen garden or from fruits gathered for free in the countryside. There surely can be nothing more pleasant than fresh baked scones served with a selection of home-made jams and jellies, eaten beside a roaring fire

on a cold winter evening, evoking memories of warm summer days and blue skies.

Bramble Jelly

---

4 lbs / 1¾ kg blackberries   sugar to taste
2 large lemons   1¾ pts / 1 litre / 4 cups water

Wash the blackberries under cold running water and remove any stalks or leaves, etc. Squeeze the lemons and put the juice, water and blackberries into a large preserving pan and simmer for about an hour, until the fruit has turned to a pulp. Strain the pulp through a jelly bag into a large bowl. Measure the liquid and to each pint add 1 lb sugar and put into a clean pan, heating it gently, stirring all the time until the sugar is dissolved. Bring to the boil and boil rapidly until setting point is reached. Skim and pot into sterilized jars, cover and label.

Lemon Curd

---

4 oz / 100 g / ½ cup sugar   2 oz / 50 g / 4 tbsp butter
1 egg   1 lemon

Grate rind from lemon, squeeze out juice. Put the butter, sugar, rind and juice into a saucepan and melt the butter slowly. Add the egg, well beaten, and stir until the mixture thickens. Pour into a sterilized jar, cover and label.

Strawberry Jam

1¾ lbs / ¾ kg / 5 cups strawberries
2¼ lbs / 1 kg / 4½ cups preserving sugar

knob of butter

Wash, dry and hull the strawberries then crush, using a potato masher (for a jam with a smoother texture you can put the fruit into a food processor). Put the crushed strawberries in a large saucepan and add the sugar. Heat very gently, stirring all the time, until the sugar dissolves. *Do not allow to boil at this stage.* Add the butter then, still stirring, increase the heat and bring to the boil, a boil that bubbles vigorously, rises in the pan and cannot be stirred down. Allow to boil for 4 minutes exactly then remove from the heat. Working quickly, pot in sterilized jars and cover with waxed paper circles, then cling film or jam covers. Label and date. Let stand in your store-cupboard for at least 3 weeks before using.

Lemonade

Served in a tall jug with ice and wafer thin slices of lemon nothing is more refreshing on a hot summer afternoon.

4 large lemons   water
6 oz / 150 g / ¾ cup caster sugar

Using a very sharp knife remove the zest from the lemon, then squeeze out all the juice into a bowl. Put the lemon zest and caster sugar into a separate bowl and pour over 2 pints / 1 litre / 5 cups boiling water, stirring all the time, until the sugar has dissolved. Leave to cool, then strain into a clean bowl and add the lemon juice. Chill well.

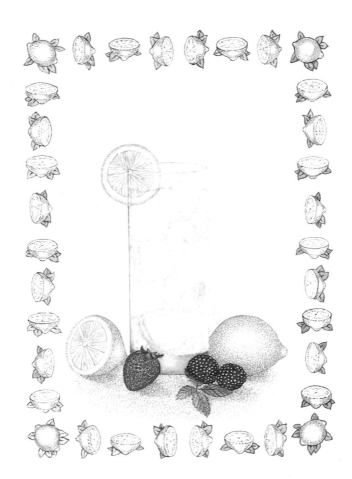

Index